MORNING BREAKS IN
THE ELEVATOR

LEMN SISSAY

MORNING BREAKS IN THE ELEVATOR

LEMN SISSAY

CANONGATE
Edinburgh · New York · Melbourne

First published in 1999 by Payback Press,
an imprint of Canongate Books Ltd,
14 High Street, Edinburgh EH1 1TE

This edition published by Canongate in 2006

2

British Library Cataloguing-in-Publication Data
A catalogue record for this book is
available upon request from the British Library.

0 86241 838 0 (10-digit ISBN)
978 0 86241 838 0 (13-digit ISBN)

Printed and bound in Great Britain by Clays Ltd, St Ives plc

FOR MY AUNT, ALEMASH STEFANOS

CONTENTS

ACKNOWLEDGEMENTS

Some of the poems in this book were commissioned for or first broadcast on *The Emma Freud Show* (BBC Radio 1, 1995); *In Living Colour* (BBC Radio 4, 1997); *A–Z* (BBC World Service, 1997); *Wham, Bam, Strawberry Jam* (BBC2, 1997); *Love Thang* (BBC Radio 4, 1997); *Kaleidoscope* (BBC Radio 4, 1998); *Stanza On Stage* (BBC World Service and BBC Radio 4, 1998); *Jazz 606* (BBC2, 1998); and *The Andrea Oliver Show* (Greater London Radio, 1999).

The poem *'Flock of Sound'* was commissioned by The National Music Network and performed (with other poems) throughout the UK in 1995 with saxophonist and composer David Murray in The David Murray UK– USA Big Band, and subsequently on BBC Radio 3 in 1996.

The poem *'Crowd Control'* is featured on the CD *One Hell of a Storm* produced by Tongue & Groove. 'Crowd Control' was first published in *Straight No Chaser* magazine.

The poems *'Colour Blind'*, *'Fair'*, and *'Invisible Kisses'* have previously been published in *The Fire People: A Collection of Contemporary Black British Poets* (Payback Press, 1998).

'Sandwich Love' and *'The Waitress'* have been published in *Poems In Your Pocket* (Longmans, 1999), and *'The Waitress'* is set to appear in *IC3: A Collection of Black British Writers* (Penguin, 2000).

'The Elevator' is a short film produced by Tigerlily Films and set for show in 2000. Thanks to producer Nikki Parrott, director Alrick Riley and The British Film Institute.

Thanks for the musicians I have worked on stage or in studio in between books: David Murray, James Spaulding, Jerry Dammers and Chris Cookson. Thanks to Gary Crosby, Kenrick Rowe, Deavid Jean Baptiste and Jonathon Gee of The Fire People. Thanks to Tony 'Tidy' Thompson, Andy Spiro, Yvonne Shelton, Liz Sharpley and Rupert Campbell of Secret Society. Thanks to Tim, Rob, Andy and Will of The Appollo Sax Quartet. Thanks to Helmut Heur of Lounge Records in Germany. Thanks to the following groups with whom I have recorded my poetry: IZIT, Leftfield, Byron Woollen Working Week and Disjam.

Thanks to Daniella Bernadelle of David Higham Associates. Thanks to live reading agent Paul Beazley of 57 Productions. Thanks to Jamie Byng and Colin McLear for their encouragement and to Whitney Byng for bridge building. Thanks to Michael Unger of The Manchester Evening News. Thanks to Nod Knowles. Thanks to Anthony H Wilson. Thanks to Lisa Berriman of Oris Watches. Thanks to all the staff at the Colombia Hotel.

Dearest thanks to my friends - you know who you are - in Britain, USA, South Africa, Ethiopia, Senegal, France and Germany. And to anyone who has had the tenacity to bear with me throughout.

I reserve the simplest and the most profound acknowledgements to both the Stefanos and Sissay families.

RECEPTION

THE WAITRESS AND THE NIGHTS OF THE ROUND TABLE

Each immaculate table a near perfect reflection of the next;
A '40s Hollywood formation dance captured in time -
In black and white.
On the mahogany, polished as a morning pond,
Each tablecloth flapped as swan's wings
And each landing perfect.
She made pieces of butter, intricate
As the hand-woven curls in a judge's wig.
And if not so legal and final
They'd be a crest of waves
Caught in yellow sunshine.

Each serviette a silent smiling signet born in her hands,
Each flower arranged as if grown for this evening
Sucks water slowly through the stem and raises its neck.
They bathe in the light flitting from cut crystal vase
And stand assertive in centre tables, waiting.
She picks a speck of dust from a spotless unspeckled carpet.
Her reflection buckles in the neck of a mercurial fork
While the solemn red candles wait
To weep their red tears.

She pauses as a mother would for a moment
In the front room, before the visitors arrive,
In admiration and slight concern
And bathes in the symmetry and silence
And the oddness of order –
Even the tables seem to brace themselves as she left.

The picture was distorted when she returned from the kitchens.
A hungry hoard of steak-sawing, wine-guzzling,
Spirit-sapping, double-breasted suits had grabbed their places.
They dug their spiked elbows into the wilting backs of tables.
The tablecloth dripped congealed red wine from its quiet hanging corners
And the sounds of their grunts, growls, their slurping,
Their gulping and tearing invaded the hall.

But a black swan amongst a sea of serrated cutlery, she soared just above
And wove a delicate determined ballet inbetween and invisible.
She walked for miles that evening, balancing platters,
Pinafore-perfect hair clipped so not to slip.
The wine warmed and the candles cried.

In the background of the lashings of laughter –
The guttural sound of wolves.
She retrieved a carcass of lamb, poured red,
And didn't notice the bloodshot eyes slide over her:
Nor the claws stretching and puncturing leather brogues;
Scratching the wooden floor; nor their irritation at her.
One mauled a mobile phone with a clumsy paw.
The alcohol-fuelled change was taking hold.
And together they could be and become who they really were.
Wolves. Wolves in their pride. Wolves in their pack.
Their lower jaws had stretched and eyes slitted –
Some even bayed as wolves, heads flicking side to side,
Tongues slipping low, slow and deliberately from their mouths
And curling sensually to their snouts. The wolf has a permanent smile.
It grew, first half-cough, half-bark. One paw banged on the table,
Another banged and another and another and another

Until the whole hall echoed with the unified clatter
Of the guttural phlegm-flicked word that brought them together
"Gerni gerni gerni gerni," they chanted. "Ggerni ggerni ggerni,"
they chanted faster. "Ggerni Ggerni Ggerni Ggerni," faster and faster.
"GgernigGerniggErnigggeRniggerNiggerNiggerNigger"

She turned to her colleagues who stood by the kitchen entrance
But their eyes! Their eyes slipped sideways away from her.
They too were wolves! Her lips parted for her voice and the room hushed itself
But for the slipping of saliva from their jaws and the flickering candles
And the dripping of the red wine from the tablecloth.
As instructed by her manager, she, smiling politely,
Asked a wolf, "More coffee sir?"

COLOUR BLIND

If you can see the sepia in the sun
Shades of grey in fading streets
The radiating bloodshot in a child's eye
The dark stains in her linen sheets
If you can see oil separate on water
The turquoise of leaves on trees
The reddened flush of your lover's cheeks
The violet peace of calmed seas

If you can see the bluest eye
The purple in the petals of the rose
The blue anger, the venom, of the volcano
The creeping orange of the lava flows
If you can see the red dust of the famished road
The white air tight strike of Nike's sign
If you can see the skin tone of a Lucien Freud
The colours of his frozen subject in mime

If you can see the white mist of the oasis
The red, white and blue that you defended
If you can see it all through the blackest pupil
The colours stretching, the rainbow suspended
If you can see the breached blue of the evening
And the caramel curls in the swirls of your tea
Why is it you say you are colour blind
When you see me?

CHARLIE'S PLAYING BLACKJACK

For David Murray

It's got to scream like a thousand shivers.
Shake down, break down, run like rivers of black fire-waves.
Rise demons and spirits from the Senegalese caves.
Rise Beloved *and* Seth! Rise the dead!
For this sound digs, digs down-down were the deep down
Is down with the deep down til it reaches the beaches of Goree.
Until it stabs-stabs as it grab-grabs the minute minute. Hold fast.
It flows through passages, right, like a flock of carrion crows
And stings and blows and stings and blows,
Makes sadness sing high and swing low.
SWEET CHARIOTS OF FIRE!

Quotes wrapped in rolled notes, stick into the spokesmen's eyes.
The hoaxmen of the mainstream deep scream.
Deep Davis deep. So deep, Davis, I can't sleep for the
Sweeping sounds of your underground. This landscape
Littered with mounds. Rise! Spirits. Rise Uncoil. Break the soil –
The bread of the dead, the salt of the earth. Rise
And flow like mercurial contours on a midnight sky. Cry.
Till the tears solidify. Fly Spirits till you become a song.
Eye to eye. Right to wrong. Untie pain. Dance again
Till juices jive down your scarred backbones.
This is the other world – *live* – and yet home.

This sound electrifies, soars on the edge of the head.
Waken the dead and tell them it's here, "it's here",
For duppies to wind and spirits to near home – at last.
To brutify then purify then reunify the past.
Rise Malcolm, the Jews, the blues and the Soledad brothers
Shout. Bleed. Breath. Heal. Shout. Breath. Heal. Bleed
I swear I saw another slave freed, its soul freed, it gather speed,
It push me over the edge of the ledge, dredging the graveyards,
the spirits – Charlie's playing cards on the tomb, a dead man's womb.

Don't you get it. It's genetic. A musical hallucinogenic. Insane –
The music of love through the instruments of pain,
Shooting from the lip, from the tip of the tongues of the wronged.
Hang on, hang on with your finger tips. Pray you don't slip
Cause we climbing the timing the landscape of mine
Turn this poem sideways it's like a New York skyline
A state of mind.

And through to the solo light. Right. Solo.
How does it go? It glides like an eagle inches from the waves
With a rush that sounds like caves should sound like.
It rips through all mind-binds, breaks all seals, tears all seems - seams,
Chilled as fresh-iced screams, angry as sweated dreams.
It bites like a baby, kicks like a dog, slicker than a card trick.
Demons spit and twist as spirits hit notes high (ha!) and snare.
This is where contrasts explode and it's natural to find
Sharpness next to curves next to shadows next to verve,
And new definitions of time. It is the blood of the vein.
The music of love through the instruments of pain.

Hot cold shy bold rock rolled blue soul. Rise!
Makes an old man young a young girl old. Rise!
It's a slick wild blast, cast from chains of slaves.

I found my jazz. Rise. I found my jazz. Rise.
I found my jazz and was saved.
Rise spirits.

INVISIBLE KISSES

If there was ever one
Whom when you were sleeping
Would wipe your tears
When in dreams you were weeping;
Who would offer you time
When others demand;
Whose love lay more infinite
Than grains of sand.

If there was ever one
To whom you could cry;
Who would gather each tear
And blow it dry;
Who would offer help
On the mountains of time;
Who would stop to let each sunset
Soothe the jaded mind.

If there was ever one
To whom when you run
Will push back the clouds
So you are bathed in sun;
Who would open arms
If you would fall;
Who would show you everything
If you lost it all.

If there was ever one
Who when you achieve
Was there before the dream
And even then believed;
Who would clear the air
When it's full of loss;
Who would count love
Before the cost.

If there was ever one
Who when you are cold
Will summon warm air
For your hands to hold;
Who would make peace
In pouring pain,
Make laughter fall
In falling rain.

If there was ever one
Who can offer you this and more;
Who in keyless rooms
Can open doors;
Who in open doors
Can see open fields
And in open fields
See harvests yield.

Then see only my face
In the reflection of these tides
Through the clear water
Beyond the river side.
All I can send is love
In all that this is
A poem and a necklace
Of invisible kisses

SLIPPING

you
are
slipping
away
Don't
Go if you want to
see if I need you

        are
        slipping
        away
        Don't
        Leave if you want to
        see if I miss you

                are
                slipping
                away
                Don't
                Call if you want to
                see If I miss you

                        slipping
                        slipping
                        Don't
                        Wave if you want to
                        see if I care for you

                                are
                                slipping
                                slipping
                                slipping
                                away

MURDERING BILL

With less than the pressure
Of a downpressing butterfly wing in a feather field -
The opening of an eyelid would make more noise -
He opened the letterbox so slowly that it was
As unsuspecting as a passing yawn in the morning.
A smooth criminal face tattooed with blue ink
With *my* name peers. This Royal Male
The silent secret stalker crouched delicately
Outside the front door – eyes filled the letterbox
Like two greedy gulping goldfish in a tank.

He drinks in the shadows of the sleeping hall
And becoming almost liquidite
Squeezes savagely through the letterbox
Arms first, head stretched, ears cut
Now he had the eyes and the body of a lizard
The strain written in blue veins on his face
 He pulls through the legs and he is in.

A lizard. He waits for breath to calm and becomes
Cold and camouflaged. Digging his elbows into carpet
He slides into the front room where I am
Enveloped in the Saturday paper. Turn a page
This is my affidavit this is what happened.
I saw him I read the look in his eyes and he read mine
He laughed at me. Stood on his hind legs and spat at me.

His tongue slipping from his mouth like a serrated ribbon.
There he is lying in the centre of my front room
He slumped from my clammy clumsy hands
Back to the floor limp. His head and legs bent
I've been here transfixed since. Staring at him
Waiting for him to die – but he breaths he breaths
As many times as I twist his damned throat he breaths.

ATTEMPTED

He measured the rope, left a note
Saying how he "couldn't take it any more".
He stood on a chair kicked it away
And landed on the floor.
So he stuck his head in the gas oven and
Groped for the gas knob.
The pan of spaghetti spilled over his neck
And he burned his hand on the hob.

I saw him walking defiantly on the motorway
Waiting, arms aloft for cars to run him over.
But the police came and they charged him
For obstructing the hard shoulder.
All in all there were no cars
To make scrap of his heart before it's time,
So he walks, defiant, blindfolded
Down a disused railway line.

IMMIGRATION RSVP

The lemons you suck are from Spain
And the orange you drink's from South Africa.
Shoes you wear are made in Pakistan
And your oil is from Saudi Arabia.

You import your petrol from the Gulf States
And your toys are made in Taiwan.
Your coffee they send from Colombia
And your cars are driven from Japan.

You've flooded yourself with foreign good
But foreigners you tell me are bad.
You say you're afraid that they'll over run you
But I'm afraid they already have.

ERRATIC EQUIPOISE

Paranoid ploughmen of the public. Post pubescent punk parasites parade as pigs. Poisonous pen pushing peace paraphrasing purile predecessors of pain. They piss on people. Proof perverts with preshrunk prostrates, preaching peace pushing pain. Primitive prozac packed protein packed pulsating pressure points. Paranoid pirhanas. Oink. An oratorial orchid of oinks. Onshore outlaws. Organisation of one sided ombudsmen. Operation Orwellian orgy. Our off offending opposite of open offensive officers ooze out of the okapis oiliest orifice. The outsiders oversetting order. Ordeal orchestrators over law over proof operators. Outcast offspring of oran-utans. Oink. Lashing lizards lacerating lives with lies. Launderers of liberty looking for lazarus. Laminated liars. Legions of labaradors love and lick the loins of loophole logic, laugh lavatorially at liberty. Its a livelihood for leftover listless layabouts, latent lawbreakers and leastways loose and limbless lightweights. Licensed loathsome lawless leeches of the legal labyrinth. Informers isolating, incriminating, innocents. Imbecilic imbalanced illywhackers. Insolent ink illusionists. Interrogators implementing ideological injustices with immeasurable intelligence and immunity to innocence. Injustice irradiant in the impermeable institution. Intimidating intolerable intonations infiltrate their ink and inhabits their iris. These insular inhibited infantile infantrymen. Challenging carthorses career carelessly in our city scape. Choreographers of chaos curators of circumstance. Chronic charlatans choking civility. Claiming clairaudience they clasp claviform clauses causing claustrophobia and crushing the chronic. Classified. Coast to coast cockroaches. Commited creaters of cobweb codes. Erratic energetic erasers of equity. Enforcers evacuating ethics employing experts in the extraction of eyes from eyewitnesses. Equality. Equal to elephant excrement. Emmersed in ego. Euqanimity evicted equality emmersed in equivocality and embroidery of explanation. Episodes of endless encounters enflame this "erratic" equipoise. Equipoise. Equipoise. Equipoise.

FAIR

I'll reign in then chain you in.
I'll slit whip and rip into you
Till all the cold as nitric acid resentment
Pours out of my black chest
Onto your purpled curdled and blistered back.
I'll whip you till you howl and crawl and cry.
I'll pour salt in your mouth, rub shit in your eyes.
Pour vinegar into the canals of your ears.
I'll verify all your superficial fears

I'll wrench each finger from each joint
Till you get my point. Get it. Get my point!
I'll drag you by the roots of your hair -
Make you wish you were no-one from nowhere.
Show you what it's like on the other side;
Show you what it's like on the far side.
My knuckle-dusted fists will rein down
Busting veins will curse,
Blow after bitter blow
I'll ask you how it feels
I'm doing a thesis, I'd really like to know

I'll cut you a thousand times
While repeating the line
"Yes I know, your blood is red like mine."
I'll rip out your wife's fallopian tubes
Cause there's already too many of you.
I'll make you drink your own hiss,

I'll make you listen to this,
One two three thousand times and more
Show you what it's like to know the score.
I'll sell drugs to your children,
Burn down your home,
Make you a stranger to your own,
And what's more
The moment you run on fire,
Through this poem, for the door
Gasping for air and some sense of pride
The same damned experience
willl waiting for you outside

I haven't finished -
When it dawns that this scorning
Is sworn in and government-approved
When the pattern starts to emerge
And you're on the verge of enlightenment or madness,
Immersed in the quiet violence of the day-to-day laws,
When you notice the holder of the mirror has claws
And the reflection provided is disfigured and displaced.
When your tongue splits on the bitter taste,
When you head implodes,
Because the text between the lines
Is so suffocating that you've started reading minds,
When all this is said and done and said and done
You may accuse me of being a racist
And that we can continue "this discussion"
On a more equal basis!

ONE LEVEL

THE REPOSSESSION: LOT 67

A girl clasped by the sinews of vicious storms
Of saliva spat through sanctimonious scorn.

Gossip gathered in teacups and tapping tea spoons
"How dare a woman bear such waste in her womb?"

They locked her in the watchtower for husbandless women
And counted her debt in the cells that were splitting.

Forced her to bathe by night in tin tubs of guilt
Or be damned to the sewer's side with the skeleton silt.

They pressured her each day to study Mary Immaculate in pastel pictures
Made her eat the dead and dry daily bread of water and scriptures.

And no sooner had the secrets of birth found her
Than the hospital curtains crept around her.

No sooner had air swilled in virgin lungs and seeped through the critical mesh
Than they thumped their fists into her and gripped their pound of flesh.

Bathed in blood. Without pressure the womb weak and depressed
Miss, the bailiff growled, your child has been repossessed.

BAPTISM IN MIRE

As the pastor dragged the 'forgiven'
From that watery grave
They'd say "Jesus Christ"
And he'd shout "You are saved."

My F. parents 'chastised' me
For the way that I frowned
They thought me possessed by the devil
I thought they were being drowned.

CONTROLLED EXPLOSIONS

Picked up in anticipation and dropped in greater disappointment
By distressed couples searching for their own intimate luggage.
The suitcase has been tampered with and rummaged through
Doesn't know where it's come from nor where it's going to.
Its dog-eared flight-tags lost in streams of weaving conveyor belts
Its broken zips open lips too tired to beg the desperate duets.
Ham-fisted and impatient they fumble inside the hammered leather
Finding in someone else's belongings an unforgiving unfamiliarity.
They wash their hands clinically forget about mending it and disappear.

As time passes the suitcase becomes battered and bruised
Stubbornly jamming the conveyor belts at the airport,
Reminding families to grip their suitcases and step politely over
Before guilt or fear sets in. Someone reports the problem
Tannoys whisper, security arrives. Order and authority descends
Causing disorder and panic amongst the passing.

This case is the lost cargo of international departures.
With broken zips and hidden padlocked dust-collecting pockets
It may explode, for all we know, at any time.
Carefully, cordons are placed around the area.
To make sure everyone is covered
All the conveyor belts grind to a mournful halt
The airport gathers quietness and a sweeping hush blows.
Outside a professional looks confidently at camera. It's news!
I've been reliably informed the controlled explosion shall begin shortly.

CHILDREN'S HOME

The children nearby came to our secret garden
Gazed at our mansion in disbelief
Either said they wished they lived here
Or that this was the den of the thief
But it was our Narnia of food fights at midnight
Wet flannel battles in the halls
Fire extinguishers that lose their heads
We had nothing to lose – nothing at all

But the rattle of rules and keys
Broke the magic – we all knew it couldn't last
The alarm bells rang and rang and rang
In Emergency Break The Glass
And it's no fun any more in here
The keys in cupboards, slamming security doors
Each child slowly retracts inside their self
Whispering "What am I being punished for?"

We'd been given booby-trapped time-bombs
Trigger wires hidden, strapped on the inside
It became a place of controlled explosions
Self-mutilation, screams and suicide
Of young people returned, return to sender
Midlit dorms of midnight's moans
We might well have all been children
But this was never a children's home

WALKING IN CIRCLES – sile innat

These compressed patches of earth.
Her footsteps deepened
And I found myself, raising my knee
To follow in them,
Raising my elbows
To climb over them,
Bracing myself
To jump in them.
Who was she
That left imprints
Deeper than myself?

Wiping sweat from the crease
Between cheek and nose
With a dirty hand I
Mumble why so deep
Wait for me.
Why so deep?

Later I realised
That without meeting
We'd been walking
In circles, stamping our imprints.
Every now and then I would
Hear her wheezing trying to climb
Over her own imprint
And jump into the next.

MY DAD IS A PILOT

My dad is a pilot. Everybody knows that.
He wore a green pilot's suit and he wore a pilot's hat.
He was never more at home, he was never more free
Than flying past the cities or skimming past the sea

He flew past the Simeon mountains, past even the stars
He flew far my dad did. He flew far.
He flew past Ethiopia of night and of day
He past my past. He flew right past
And then he passed away.

GUILT

Cold winds have frozen us
walls of fear closed on us.

The sky has fallen down on us
and fear it has frowned on us.

The lightning hasdumbfounded us
a dust cloud surrounded us.

The rain it pours down on us
pain has been found on us.

Secrets they have bound us
annointed and then crowned us.

Whispers race around us
fingers point down on us.

Fists beat and pound on us
our reflections astound us.

Fear it compounds us
defences surround us.

Frustrations hound us
guilt has found us.

LEVEL TWO

SANDWICH LOVE

Triangular sandwiches lounge on plates
They don't guffaw, gawp or gesticulate
They kiss each other lip to salivating lip
They don't posture pose and stylishly sip
They don't have calling cards and though well-dressed
Have no need or will for public address
They just pout at each other, smile and wink
They go down well with drink

Triangular sandwiches all love-struck
Have you ever seen a more glazed blushing cook?
"Slap me with the salmon and pull down the shutters"
"Smother me in butter," another one mutters
"Stroke me down with cucumber slices…"
"I like it like that, pepper me with spices,"
"Massage that cream cheese over my chest"
"Let your olive oil seep through my bread vest"

Triangular sandwiches soaked in salad dressing
The lusciously laid lovers among the depressing
Pretenders pretending they're enjoying the chat
Of the who's who in the what's what of where it must be at
The lush lounge lizards lay and like when lovers undo
Stretch by the rosed radish as corks seductively unscrew
But a suit will saunter his hand, will swoop limply from above
He will open his salivating mouth push one in and shove
He will crunch her inside his grating teeth
And leave the other sandwich sandwiched in grief

CROWD CONTROL (UK 79–97)

Winter opens the cracks where poverty pours slow and thick.
This is a soup kitchen society. Waiter, I need a truth pick.
There's less food on our plates and we forgot how to complain.
There's no jobs and yet millions to train.
Taxi drivers bite their lips and wait for tips to a better life
Or pray that you may not be so poor as to exchange cash for a knife.
Industry grovels to the stock exchange –
How can someone be so wrong and there be no-one to blame?
This is bleaker than the tranquilliser taken by the teenager,
More impersonal than the telephone pager.
It's darker than the serial killers serialised in the papers.
It's a busman's holiday for bailiffs.
They can visit their neighbours and get the job done too.
It's maybe then you realise how much you need your country
And how much your country needs of you.

There's so many working on our behalf and so little work being done
They try to persuade us that it's pratical to soak up the sea with a sponge.
They offer magician's manifestos proving night to be day –
I thought this train was moving until the other moved away.
The more dissatisfied you become the more clipboards tap on your doors.
They want your name, your number, your dna and maybe a little more.
And politicians like penguins who relish this freezing cold
Sell us bare necessities as if they were gold.
They give us free Euro comparisons, figures and think-tank statistics
So we may forget reality yet cherish what they predict.
You are naked in winter, blind and exposed.
The emperor in wisdom shares with us his new clothes.

He offers mortgages on homes built in sand
With fittings from the mirages of never-never land.

But it's when the walls feel as if they're closing in
And you try to close your eyes but your eyelids are too thin.
Maybe it's when your wife is ill and you can't afford the operation
And the doctor stops in the middle and says that's your allocation.
Or the insurance company hauls you in court for dishonest declaration
Which you made to pay for your daughter to get a decent education.
Or when your car is reclaimed because it was never really yours
And you find yourself hiding again cause someone's knocking down your door.
It's a busman's holiday for the bailiffs
They can visit the neighbours and get the job done too.
Maybe then you'll realise how much you need your country
And how much you're country needs of you!

THE ELEVATOR

It was embarrassing for him. I sixth-sensed it. Me.
One hotel. One elevator. One world. Two People.
One black. One white. One young. One old.
One thousand conflicting thoughts.
One silence. One destination.
For one it was a short journey
For one it was long.
With one nervy question
He just had to break the silence.
"Are you with the basketball team?"
I answer choosing a two-lettered
One syllable staccato reply
"No."

As he mentally rocked to and fro swilling in discomfort
The elevator hummed like it was listening into the atmosfear,
Instead of thinking that I might slam dunk his head through
A hoop that had spit for a net, I drift
I imagine the elevator gracefully passing the ground floor.
As an eagle might pass a parachutist
Who couldn't find his rip chord
It continues to go down deeper and deeper
Down where the deeper down is.
Where deep is down with deeper down.
Down.

And cool as a criminal who had stopped running
And hangs on the corner of the main street
As if his heart wasn't trying to dive
From his chest and hide in the gutter –
Cool like that – the lift stopped. And here we are.
The two of us and one magnificent silence
Broken by the chocolate New York lift voice
"You are down in the deep, the underground
Down where the deep is down with deeper down."

The elevator doors opened –
Like the curtains of the Apollo in Harlem.
The doors opened
Like the opening arms of a southern preacher.
The doors opened
Like the ebonised arms of the Ethiopian running through the winning tape.
The doors opened
And a congregation of light stretched out
Out into the room, the hall, the aerodrome.
Crept out and it poured out and it swept out and light-leapt out,
Over a sea of gold toothed bandana wrapped tatooed Nike wearing
Caterpillar booted, hip hop jumping head wrapped head shorn
Head locked swaying Gucci-strapped Armani jean wearing
Cocoa butter smelling beautiful black men and women.
Almond eyes glinting with whisky phat phunk and fumes.
The exact time that the lift doors had opened
Was the exact time that the music, mid-song, had stopped

All heads turned slowly to the intrusive source of light.
Hundreds of them. Hundreds and thousands and maybe a million.
The sweet still air was filled
With the black breath of my silent brothers and sisters,
Who did nothing more than blink and watch and register.

It was so silent that I could hear
A glorious curl of sweat abseil down his face
I could hear it fatally explode on the floor
And bounce back in the shape of a crown. Jeez!
His shaken forearm rose slowly with the lump in his throat
And his finger travelled through the thick air,
Towards the elevator lift panels.
Until finally he pressed the button for
Reception! Reception! Reception!

A FLOCK OF SOUND

There is a rhythm, a soul's rhythm
A come in from the cold rhythm,
A no need to go rhythm,
A take of your bruise shoes
And shake off tomorrow rhythm,
There is a rhythm, a wild rhythm,
An adult's just a child rhythm,
A blissed out whispering
Smile while listening rhythm.

There is a rhythm, a higher than sky rhythm,
The rhythm of spaces, a sweet tasting,
Liquor laced rhythm. An eyelid flicking
Slick thigh licking rhythm.
A come home to the comfort zone rhythm.
A relax in your black take nothing back rhythm.

There is a rhythm. A rhythm.
A sweet sounding grounded rhythm,
A spaced out sense of place rhythm,
A 'give in to your within' rhythm,
A rainy season body teasing
Dripping sugar caned cocooned,
Landing on the moon rhythm.
A making room rhythm.

A lake and mist lip kissing dew glistening
Earthed and wired surround sound future bound
Magic carpeted and homeward bound rhythm
A pain soothing hip moving pressure releasing
Depression decreasing graffiti wriggling baby
Giggling zebra crossing – Walk don't walk – button pressing
Up town down town dressing spirit shaking earth quaking
Ripples in a lake of a rhythm
Ripples in a lake of a rhythm
Ripples in a lake.
A flock of sound.

LOVE & THE BLENDER

We don't give each other small pebbles
Flowers picked from the park
Or next door's garden.

Measuring gifts by cost
There lays the price of love
Lost in that wasted time.

There are no surprise visits
No piggy backs, no silly voiced telephone calls
No love letters.

There is no lifting of veils
We suck all the air in each others presence
And writhe on the front room floor for it.

Indifferent. Rooms.
We silently hope for each other
To lose a finger or two in the blender
So love might shine through pity.

THE GRADUATE AND HER SECRET THESIS

It was the evening before the eve of her deadline.
They made love between the sheets of her thesis.
After taking a shower of words she sat at the table
And studied him through the book pile, turned over leaves;
She perfected paragraphs punctuated with references,
Glue to stick the whole thing together. 2,500 words to go.

In her mind she had passed the exam already
But at the same time her pencil snapped
Like the cracking of a twig signifies an intruder
A problem. It stalked her thoughts, scared her
That stubborn sentence if not justified would turn into a tapeworm, a
   gremlin
Eat the whole thesis and belch in her face
We engaged and I followed her delicate fingers
Along that snare riddled trigger wired sentence.
She read it again and again in the voice of a question
Finding new angles, each time and new meanings
That refer to previous explanations in other books
That neither of us had at the time –
She stared at me for the answer and I at her
This was going to take work – more work than either expected
Midnight.

In the whisk of a page, the thud of a dropped book
We entered the old university reference library
The closing doors behind us sent
A gust of air dust curling and searching

Down the corridors of books like a flock of grey swans
The night light shone a red brown
I noticed how different she looked – nervous almost
Her caramel skin more beautiful than usual
I've since forgotton who'd said let's split up and search but we did.

THE HAND THAT FEEDS ME

You slit my face with whips made of dried veins.
Twist and tie these blue hands behind my back.
My damned spirit bruised splattered with blood stains.
Shadows now I fear are devils in black.
You broke in and choked me filled my throat with soot.
Forced choices of devils or deep seas.
You scoured these ebony wrists with cuts.
Flung me from bridges, hung me from dead trees.
You have scarred me, hounded me through my dreams.
Poured a scale of wet salt around my heart.
In quiet moments that you fill with screams
I burn inside and claw my self apart
As I rise from water – Your reflection!
You near drowned me in your imperfection.

INNER CITY OUT OF MY MIND

Another day flies
Another brother dies
Another mother haunts
Her home with her own cries.
Another man falls
To another chant and call
From another racist neighbour
Behind another thin wall.

Another sleeps well
Through another night of hell –
Another tranquillizer
And no-one will tell
That yet another dream
Was not what it seemed
More a paper veil
For a hollow of screams.

Another sister flies
From the building in the sky
Clutching another catalogue
Of clothes she couldn't buy.
Anohther suicide
Another broken inside
Another written letter
For the parents to hide.

Another dream shatters
As another man batters
The hope from the eyes
Of a woman of matters.
Another crack alarm
Another track in the arm
Another vein hides from
Another shot of calm.

Every day living
Every day I give in
Every day I wake up
To a new beginning.

THE FALLING SUMMER

Bette: 1955–1997

I will not fall into fall on the breeze of grief
Pushed slightly to me from your last breath.
I will not let winter dull the memory
That you so caringly carefully left
I cannot leave you roses each day
But will lay down fresh dew each night.
I will leave you love in each leaf of fall
And each dawn a bed of light.

A READING IN STANSTEAD

I reckoned there must have been a bad smell in the air
Because the bar man had a 'what's that smell' look to him.
I'd travelled two hundred and fifty miles to get here.
I put on my amiable one, and asked for the manager.
The landlord with a frown yawned.
His upper lip stretched to the ceiling
And his lower sloped slovenly to the floor and
His lips slapped back together like a slow gospel handclap.
Some dribble hung and unravelled on to the floor
His eyes clung to his face to stop them slipping down his cheeks.
Wet, hairy and matted dog's legs sprawled from his shoulders
And he paddled unstable in the air. He scuttled clumsily off the stool
And lapped at the bowl of water on the floor
Keeping one pathetic eye on me. A little odd I thought.

I looked to the x-ray eyed barmaid –
Everyone was a little too undisturbed for comfort.
It was as if a known gangster had just arrived.
She was rooted to the spot
Looking alternately at me and through me.
Her smile twitched and twitched again.
First the left side, then the right then the left
Then both sides twitching and twitching.
I stepped back as her sweet top lip began to uncurl upwards
Splitting at the lip edges and peeling over her nose.
The skin trembled, rippled, and ripped itself back overhead
Until a deflated mould of her face and hair flapped on her back from her neck.
Still rooted, she screamed in a deep voice.

Desperately, I guessed, trying to keep her head on.
I couldn't quite put my finger on it
But something was definitely wrong here.
Something had disturbed this olde English pub
The smattering of locals were staring at somebody
Who must have been stood near me. They ogled.
The mirror behind the bar became a cluster of fascinated faces.

As contracted I began reading my poetry
But the air thickened around my words
As if I'd bruised it. Each syllable floated before my eyes.
A big, fat, pink woman with purple circles around her eyes.
Rose through the air. She began to panic and doggy paddle,
But it was too late and she was sucked through the window.
There was either too much pressure on the outside or on the inside.
The room was crammed with words waiting to be received
Dying wilting words fighting for air, clutching their necks on the carpet
Clawing themselves up walls, staggering at the bar.

The outside air bolted through me, like wild horses, gallopped and turned.
I bathed in it for a while before diving into the taxi –
The taxi driver was a wolf too.
I took a glimpse back through the oranged window.
The barmaid flirted. The manager sucked on his cigar.
And the locals grappled with each other's English tales of intrigue.
Good, I thought, a real country pub. At least the gangster has gone.

THE BRUISE

I got the bruise, the bruise,
Since before I was born.
Bruise is the only clothing
That I've ever worn.

I got the bruise, the bruise,
Nothing no doctor can do.
Don't come near me woman
Cause I'm sure gonna bruise you too.

I got the bruise in my flesh
The bruise deep and dark.
I got the bruise all over my face, my arms
my head, my soul 'n' my heart

I get so drunk I get bruises on my bruise
And that ain't no disguise.
I got the bruise, I got the bruise
I got the bruise in my eyes.
I got the bruise, I got the bruise
I got the bruise in my eyes.

QUIET PLACES

Some people on bus seats, shake at the shoulders,
Stoned Elvises trying to dance after the gig

Some walk into the rain and look like they're smiling
Running mascara writes sad bitter letters on their faces

Some drive their cars into lay-bys or park edges
And cradle the steering-wheel looking like headless drivers

Some sink their open mouths into feather pillows
And tremble on the bed like beached dolphins

Some people are bent as question marks when they weep
And some are straight as italic exclamation marks

Some are soaking in emotional dew when they wake
Salt street maps etched into their faces.

Some find rooms and fall to the floor as if praying to Allah. Noiseless
Faces contorted in that silent scream that seems like laughter

Why is there not a tissue-giver? A man who looks for tears
Who makes the finest silk tissues and offers them free?

It seems to me that around each corner beneath each stone
Are humans quietly looking for a place to cry on their own

WINDOWSTILL

It's the lightbulb, a swinging buddha above mentally disabled shadows.
The skirting-boards freeze in fear of blame – backs up against the walls –
And wait in silence for detectives to draw a dry digit,
And point to the evidence that no one but no one has been here for weeks.
Magnifying pebbles of solidified breath stick to the window.
They've no respect for the moment and dance down the pane.
They settle on the sill and nudge nervously towards the edge.
A cautious crowd of waiting water has gathered there.

And on the mantlepiece above the fire the page of an open book, drying,
Turns itself over a day or two and lies like an unfinished post-mortem,
Waiting to be fingered and mauled, to be studied and frowned upon,
Then slid cold on a shelf with the others. Stone read.
The fading digital clock squints. The tap drips on the kitchen sink.
A fly fights in the crowd on the sill with sporadic spasms until,
Its wings sodden with struggle its struggle suddenly with wings, still.

LEVEL FREE

MOURNING BREAKS

They always said I was over the edge
And now I am. I really am over the edge!
But as I dropped in a gasp of air I grasped a branch.
That, I hoped, had its roots in the rock or rock solid roots
But there's a breeze blowing, a stunning storm coming
Thickening ink spills and swills on a bleating paper sky
A crowd of rain on the horizon staggers nearer
I sway so. I know so. I slip a little more
I know so I sway so. I grip a little more.
These tender fingers in a clenched fist
I must have slit my back. It hurts like a howl.
It stings like a scowl, weeps and stings again.
The skin splitting and spitting from my spine sides
And a pain develops muscles that create mouths
That simulate sounds of whole cities screaming.
There's a storm coming. A coming storm.
Dust spits from the cliff top into my river-eyes
Forcing tears over the banks to flood me.
I will not drown in them. I will not drown.
I am hanging on. I am hanging on. I am hanging on.

In the zip of a thick ribbon of wind
A god or a devil appears floating in front of me
And tells me in a hunch of a NY accent
"Let go, let go - Death is just the beginning
Of the end of the beginning of the end..."
And continued for forty one days and forty one nights
"Of the end of the beginning of the end of the End..."

And in a crack of lightning the devil or the god vanished.
Nothing more to concentrate on. But a storm
The sky. And my breaching back. And the cliff
And the edge. And the uprooting branch.
And my knuckles so sore cracked and numb
They favour a knot of bleeding wood.
If I look down (and I do look down) I see
That blood has poured from my back; seeped
Along the smoothness of my backside. Slid under
My testicles and coiled its way seductively
Around my thighs, knees and ebonised legs
It pours in abundance from my feet and skydives
I watch these red tears fall for ever and transform
Into explicit flowers as they reach the floor
I will not become one. I am hanging on.
I am hanging on. I am hanging on.

Whispers from above me. From above me whispers gather
The cliff ledge lined with edgy people of all colours
Some humming "Amazing graze" others simply staring
Some I saw pointing at my back and wincing.
A bearded man with his hand on a bible or a red book or a white book
Or a leather book or a revolutionary book or a dark green book
Shouted down to me in Sermonic tones deeper than the sea
"Let go. In the name of God. Let go!!"
A nervous follower peeps down and offers the advice that
"There's someone down there, they'll catch you"
And before I get chance to answer they erupt into a sky shattering
"Someone's Crying Lord – Let Go. Someone's Crying Lord – Let Go"
The harmony of those collected voices woke the spirit of the sky

And they threw crosses at me. It's raining crosses.
I look down past my feet – a devil or a god
A man the size of a pea is mouthing the words "Let go"
Night-time was approaching. Breathless I whispered.
I will not fall. Never have. Never will. Not fall. Not fall.
But as quick as they came to help is as quick as they were gone.
But I am hanging on. I am hanging on. I am hanging on.

Darkness cloaked the horror of night-time
Of gangerous spirits that fed upon open wounds.
As lightning struck I saw glimpses of their faces;
Demons whose countenance had slipped;
Whose fingers had stretched and nails had curled
Whose breath stank so viciously that I spewed to the sea
(My mamtra I am hanging on I am hanging on I am hanging on)
Throughout the darkness and fear until sunrise. And the stillness of

Morning breaking. I was a silhouette hanging from a branch
Against the chalky cliff. Only the sound of my trickling blood,
My breaking back and the moaning sky for comfort.
My shadow stretching across the cliff like a script title
On handmade paper.
The sulking storm retreated into the horizon to recollect –
Even the sea is trying to throw off its reflection.
I listened more, to the tearing of my backflesh as I hang
The flapping wet skin of my bloodied back as it hangs
Tears painted salt veins along my ebonised skin.
As that stark sunlight skidded across a bloodied sky
I sensed the presence of two symmetrical shadows descending.
They stretched seemingly even pushing back the clouds

I felt them push warm air into my face.

I saw them in the corner of each of my eyes. Magnificent wings

And felt the new muscles of my back and my chest expand with air.

Further and further. New Air. New spirit. And there with not a soul around me

I unpeeled my tender, fingers from that dew drenched branch

I let the sun pour into my eyes and finally after years I let go. Why?

Because I was growing. I was growing wings all the time. And I can fly.

MESSAGES FROM THE MINDS OF MY BROTHERS AND SISTERS

Messages From The Minds Of My Brothers And Sisters

As long as you think of yourself as a target someone will take aim. Once you stop thinking of yourself as a target it is then you can take aim at those who would've took aim at you.

Messages From The Minds Of My Brothers And Sisters

Your identity is the place you travel outwards from but they will keep on asking you to return to it, to justify it – for whom? They call this "integration".

Messages From The Minds Of My Brothers And Sisters

When you are weak it is only the weaker that gain confidence from this.

Messages From The Minds Of My Brothers And Sisters

The worst thing about paranoia in the black man is that more often than not his visions are absolutely right – he just hasn't learned to ignore them.

Messages From The Minds Of My Brothers And Sisters

Parents tell us that to climb out of the ghetto, we must work twice as hard but can't bring themselves to tell us that if we fall, we fall twice as hard.

Messages From The Minds Of My Brothers And Sisters

Have we been waiting to be accepted for so long that not being accepted has become the criteria for our acceptance?

Messages From The Minds Of My Brothers And Sisters

I never knew I lived in a ghetto until I read it in the news.

Messages From The Minds Of My Brothers And Sisters

Speak your mind or lose it.

Messages From The Minds Of My Brothers And Sisters

We define our individual sanity by how well we can articulate or understand our collective madness.

Messages From The Minds Of My Brothers And Sisters

You can't keep receiving blows to the face (without responding) because you are searching for the person who won't do it. If there is a strong flair towards racism in society then there is nothing wrong or racist about the generalisation that this society is racist.

Messages From The Minds Of My Brothers And Sisters

I see many people separating from me, standing one step backwards away from me. Then they point their accusing fingers at me and they proclaim "are you integrating or separating or what!"

Messages From The Minds Of My Brothers And Sisters

What is institutionalised racism, but a whole lot of racist individuals inside an institution blaming the institution for its racism.

Messages From The Minds Of My Brothers And Sisters

Anger is the ultimate expression for the search for love and understanding.

Messages From The Minds Of My Brothers And Sisters

How many times must I hear people say love is all we need. They say this as they take babies from other cultures. Love on its own kills and suffocates. Love is only made safe when mixed with understanding.

•

PERFORMANCE POETRY?

If Lemn Sissay's live audience is moved by his work – and he loves reading live – this does not equate with his readings being a "performance". He believes the description (in its everyday usage) implies an act. And an act implies an untruth. Indeed it is often used as a disingenuous accolade, particularly in Britain. To truly see the misapplication of the term simply look at its supposed opposite (or supposed opponent) – 'Page Poetry'. Lemn Sissay believes this too to be a bizarre banal non-descript term and can find neither page nor performance poetry in the *Princeton Encyclopedia of Poetry and Poetics*. Whether the audience is moved, angered, in laughter or in tears at one of his readings it is by no means a performance! In fact, that is what makes it special. This same assertion is documented as far back as 1988 on The Spoken Word release 'Blackvibe' by Lemn Sissay.

"Lemn Sissay has success written on his forehead." Guardian

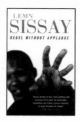

Rebel Without Applause
by
Lemn Sissay

Lemn Sissay's poems are laid into the streets of downtown Manchester, feature on the side of a public house in the same city and have been emblazoned on a central London bus route.

He has been published in press as diverse as the *Times Literary Supplement* and the *Independent*, *The Face* and *Dazed & Confused*.

He has been commissioned to write poetry, documentaries and plays for Radio 1 and Radio 4, as well as being involved in television in the roles of writing, performing and presenting.

He is published in over sixty books and features on the Leftfield album *Leftism*.

Rebel Without Applause is the stunning debut collection that started it all for Lemn Sissay.

"The product of an imagination that is rare, passionate, committed, occasionally distraught, funny and tender" *Straight No Chaser*

"In Sissay's work, we witness declamation being honed and brought to a fine art. This volume of poetry established his reputation as an extremely accomplished poet" Valerie Bloom

"Fierce, funny, serious, satirical, streetwise and tender." *Big Issue*

1 84195 001 7 (10-digit ISBN)
978 1 84195 001 3 (13-digit ISBN)

£7.99 pbk
Or buy direct from: www.canongate.net

"A wonderful subversion of cultural myths." Time Out

Transformatrix
by
Patience Agbabi

From Hamburg to Jo'burg, Oslo to Soho, Patience Agbabi follows her critically acclaimed debut collection *R.A.W.* with *Transformatrix*, an exploration of women, travel and metamorphosis.

Inspired by '90s poetry, '80s rap and '70s disco, *Transformatrix* is a celebration of literary form and constitutes a very potent and telling commentary on the realities of modern Britain.

It is also a self-portrait of a poet whose honesty, intelligence and wit manages to pack a punch, draw a smile and warm your heart – all at once.

"A rising star." *Observer*

"Patience Agbabi is only more proof that great performance poetry can bring to the page that raw, wicked stuff that has brought British poetry back to life."
Benjamin Zephaniah

"Her ideas are both originally and beautifully expressed. Or angrily expressed. Or spat out with sharp humour, always touching a nerve. And she can write and perform almost hypnotically." *Diva*

0 86241 941 7 (10-digit ISBN)
978 0 86241 941 7 (13-digit ISBN)

£7.99 pbk

Or buy direct from: www.canongate.net